BERTRAND RUSSELL

Common Sense
and
Nuclear Warfare

SIMON AND SCHUSTER · NEW YORK · 1959

MANUFACTURED IN THE UNITED STATES OF AMERICA
LITHOGRAPHED BY THE MURRAY PRINTING CO.,
FORGE VILLAGE, MASS.

PREFACE

The aim of this book is to show possible means of achieving peace in ways which should be equally acceptable to Communist Nations, to NATO Nations and to uncommitted Nations. It is my hope that there is no word in the following pages suggesting a bias towards either side. What my opinions are concerning the merits of Eastern and Western political and economic systems, I have often stated, but opinions on these issues are not relevant in discussion of the dangers of nuclear warfare. What is needed is not an appeal to this or that -ism, but only to common sense. I do not see any reason why the kind of arguments which are put forward by those who think as I do should appeal more to one side than to the other or to Left-Wing opinion more than to that of men of conservative outlook. The appeal is to human beings, as such, and is made equally to all who hope for human survival.

CONTENTS

INTRODUCTION

It is surprising and somewhat disappointing that movements aiming at the prevention of nuclear war are regarded throughout the West as Left-Wing movements or as inspired by some -ism which is repugnant to a majority of ordinary people. It is not in this way that opposition to nuclear warfare should be conceived. It should be conceived rather on the analogy of sanitary measures against epidemics. The peril involved in nuclear war is one which affects all mankind and one, therefore, in which the interests of all mankind are at one. Those who wish to prevent the catastrophe which would result from a large-scale H-bomb war are not concerned to advocate the interests of this or that nation, or this or that class, or this or that continent. Their arguments have nothing whatever to do with the merits or demerits of Communism or Democracy. The arguments that should be employed in a campaign against nuclear weapons are such as should appeal, with equal force, to Eastern and Western blocs and also to uncommitted nations, since they are concerned solely with the welfare of the human species as a whole and not with any special advantages to this or that group.

It is a profound misfortune that the whole question of nuclear warfare has become entangled in the age-old conflicts of power politics. These conflicts are so virulent and so passionate that they produce a widespread inability to understand even very obvious matters. If we are to think wisely about the new problems raised by nuclear weapons, we must learn to view the whole matter in a quite different way. It must be viewed, as some new epidemic would be viewed, as a common peril to be met by concerted action.

Let us take an illustration. Suppose that a sudden outbreak of rabies occurred among the dogs of Berlin. Does anybody doubt that Eastern and Western authorities in that city would instantly combine to find measures of extirpating the mad dogs? I do not think that either side would argue: 'Let us let the dogs lose in the hope that they will bite more of our enemies than of our friends; or, if they are not to be let completely loose, let them be muzzled with easily detachable muzzles and paraded on leashes through the streets so that, if at any moment the "enemy" should let loose its mad dogs, instant retaliation would follow.' Would the authorities of East or West Berlin argue that 'the other side' could not be trusted to kill its mad dogs and that, therefore, 'our side' must keep up the supply as a deterrent? All this is fantastically absurd and would obviously not occur to anybody as a sane policy, because mad dogs are not regarded as a decisive force in power politics. Unfortunately, nuclear weapons are regarded, quite mistakenly, as capable of securing victory in war; and because they are so regarded, few men think of them in a manner consonant with sanity or common sense.

Let us take a, perhaps, more apt illustration. In the fourteenth century the Black Death swept over the Eastern hemisphere. In Western Europe it destroyed about half the population, and in all likelihood it was about equally destructive in Eastern Europe and in Asia. In those days, there did not exist the scientific knowledge necessary to combat the epidemic. In our day, if there were a threat of such a disaster, all civilized nations would combine to combat it. No one would argue, 'Perhaps this pestilence will do more harm to our enemies than to us'. Anybody who did so argue would be considered a monster of inhumanity. And yet neither the Black Death nor any similar pestilence has ever offered as terrible a threat as is offered by the danger of nuclear war. The countries of NATO, the countries of the Warsaw Pact, and the uncommitted countries have precisely the same interest in this question. The same interest, in fact, as they would have in combating a new Black Death. If this were realized by the statesmen and populations of East and West, many difficulties which now seem insuperable, or nearly so, would disappear. I am, of course, supposing that the point of view which I am advocating would be adopted by both sides equally. Given a sane and sober consideration of what is involved, this harmony on the problems of nuclear weapons would inevitably result. It would not be necessary to invoke idealistic motives, although they could be validly invoked. It would be necessary only to appeal to motives of national self-interest.

If Brinkmanship Continues

In this chapter I propose to consider the probable course of events if present policies continue without actually causing a nuclear war. This subject has been investigated in an admirable report sponsored by The National Planning Association of America: *1970 Without Arms Control; Implications of Modern Weapons Technology;* by NPA Special Project Committee on Security Through Arms Control; Planning Pamphlet No. 104; May 1958, Washington, D.C. This report has the merit of being produced by men who are not concerned in any anti-nuclear campaign, but are merely engaged in producing a picture of facts and probabilities as impartial and objective as is humanly possible. Although it proceeds on the hypothesis, which I also am adopting in the present chapter, that no great war will break out during the period in question, it admits, what is indeed obvious, that while present policies continue there is at every moment a certain likelihood of war. It says, 'not only does the danger of war remain a possibility, but the probability totalled over time increases, becoming a certainty if sufficient time elapses without succeeding in finding alternatives'. It follows that, while present policies continue, there will be constant fear of large-scale war and, as the facts become better known, this fear will increase. Increasing fear will lead to increasing armaments involving increasing expenditure and increasing rigidity of the social structure with continually diminished liberty. Only a constant propaganda of hate and terror will induce populations to accept the burdens involved. And with every year that passes, technical advances will make war, if it should come, more and more disastrous. Such a situation may, among the saner elements of the population, produce a desire for secure peace, but, in the majority, it is more likely to produce an insane horror of the 'enemy' and a state of nerves making an explosion seem less dreadful than continued apprehension.

The expenditure on armaments is, at the present time, incomparably higher than it has ever been before. According to the above-mentioned Report, the United States is now spending 45 billion dollars per annum on military preparation. 'In the United States about 10 per cent of gross national product is now devoted to military purposes. It is estimated that 15 per cent of the gross national product of the Soviet Union is similarly devoted.' If the world goes on as it is, neither better nor worse, it is estimated that, from the present time till 1970, from 1,500 to 2,000 billion dollars will have been spent on armaments, but this will certainly prove to be an underestimate, since new inventions will necessitate increasingly expensive weapons. We cannot tell what new discoveries will be made, but we can be pretty certain that there will be such discoveries. Some of them might be fairly cheap: for example, methods of bacteriological warfare. It should be possible to poison the Mississippi and the Volga, and thereby to render uninhabitable all the regions depending on water from those rivers. If a suitable method of delivery of bacteria were discovered, immense damage could be done with rather little expenditure. But most of the novelties to be expected cannot cause death so cheaply. Take, for example, control of the weather. The philosophers of Laputa reduced rebellious provinces to obedience by causing the shadow of their island to plunge the rebels into perpetual night. It should become possible, before very long, to secure that some large enemy region should have either too much or too little rain, or that its temperature should be lowered to a point where it would no longer produce useful crops. It may also become possible to melt the Polar ice and, thereby, submerge large regions which are only slightly above sea level. Such measures, however, are not yet possible, but there are others, both more terrible and even more expensive, which have lately entered the domain of feasible lunacy.

The creation of satellites has given pleasure to schoolboys and statesmen, marred only, for the West, by the fact that the first satellite was Russian. As yet, satellites are small; but it is not to be supposed that they will remain so. They do not at present carry weapons of offence, but militarists everywhere hope that they will carry such weapons before long. By means of electronic computers, they can be timed to rain death upon enemy regions, while suspending this useful activity during their passage over friendly territory. Such weapons will be enormously expensive, but on each side it will be argued: 'if the enemy may have them, we must set about having them too.'

Nor is it only satellites that are in prospect. Any day,

one side or the other may fire a projectile which will reach the moon. It is confidently expected that, before very long, it will be possible to land human beings on the moon. I have read a Russian book—and I have no doubt there are similar American books—intended for the edification of the young, which set forth carefully the conditions to be fulfilled if people are to be able to live on the moon, and even went so far as to suggest that, in time, a lunar atmosphere might be created. The tone of this book was the reverse of warlike. It was concerned to stimulate the love of adventure and the hope of scientific triumph over material obstacles. But I am afraid that it is from baser motives that Governments are willing to spend the enormous sums involved in making space-travel possible. General Putt, in evidence before the House Committee on Armed Services, explained that the United States Air Force aims at establishing a missile base on the moon, and considered that a war-head will be fired from the moon to the earth without any enormous expenditure of energy, since the moon has no atmosphere and little gravity. He declared that the moon 'might provide a retaliation base of considerable advantage over earthbound nations'. He pointed out that an attack upon the moon by the USSR would have to be launched a day or two before an attack upon the terrestrial United States if the United States was to be unable to retaliate from the moon. Such a preliminary attack upon the moon, he considered, would warn Americans of their danger. If, on the other hand, the Russians did not demolish the United States lunar installations, it would be possible, from these installations, to destroy Russia although the terrestrial United States had been obliterated. His testi-

mony was re-enforced by Richard E. Horner, Assistant
Secretary of the Air Force for Research and Development,
who saw in the establishment of lunar bases an opportunity of breaking through the nuclear stalemate. It is
curious, and typical of militarist mentality everywhere,
that both these two eminent gentlemen seemed at first
loath to admit the possibility of Russia, also, installing
missile stations in the moon. It is obvious that what one
side can do, the other, also, can do, and the only result of
such plans, if they are carried out, must be warfare *in*
the moon. General Putt, it is true, did, in the end,
acknowledge that what the United States can do in the
moon, Russia can also do, but the moral which he drew
was that the United States must also occupy Mars and
Venus which, apparently, he considered to be beyond
the reach of the Soviets. All this curious speculation
received much less publicity than might have been
expected, and I should not have known of it but for the
fact that it was reported in *I. F. Stone's Weekly* of
October 20, 1958. I have seen no account of similar plans
by the Soviet Government, but it must be assumed that
such plans exist.

In reading of the plans of militarists, I try very hard
to divest myself for the time being of the emotions of
horror and disgust. But when I read of plans to defile
the heavens by the petty squabbles of the animated lumps
that disgrace a certain planet, I cannot but feel that the
men who make these plans are guilty of a kind of impiety.
It is easy to imagine a Congressional election, or a Soviet
party dispute, turning on the question whether Americans on the moon have exterminated the Russians there
or vice versa. Such plans degrade the heavenly bodies

and the majestic course of nature to the petty stature of furious men quarrelling over trifles. But I fear it cannot be doubted that, unless our disputes are brought within reasonable proportions, the populations of the most powerful nations and their followers will be willing to reduce themselves to starvation level in the search for means of injuring each other.

Our planet cannot persist on its present courses. There may be war, as a result of which all or nearly all will perish. If there is not war, there may be assaults on heavenly bodies, and it may well happen that means will be found to cause them to disintegrate. The moon may split and crumble and melt. Poisonous fragments may fall on Moscow and Washington or on more innocent regions. Hate and destructiveness, having become cosmic, will spread madness beyond its present terrestrial confines. I hope, though with much doubt, that some gleams of sanity may yet shine in the minds of statesmen. But the spread of power without wisdom is utterly terrifying, and I cannot much blame those whom it reduces to despair.

But despair is not wise. Men are capable, not only of fear and hate, but also of hope and benevolence. If the populations of the world can be brought to see and to realize in imagination the hell to which hate and fear must condemn them on the one hand, and, on the other, the comparative heaven which hope and benevolence can create by means of new skills, the choice should not be difficult, and our self-tormented species should allow itself a life of joy such as the past has never known.

CHAPTER II

If Nuclear War Comes

There are a great many people who, having realized that a nuclear war would be a disaster, have convinced themselves that it will not occur. I profoundly hope that they are right, but if they are, it will only be because the Great Powers adopt new policies. While present policies continue on both sides, there is much more possibility of a nuclear war than is thought by the general public. The reason for the danger is that leading statesmen on both sides believe, or profess to believe, that their side might secure a victory in the old-fashioned sense. Mr Dulles warned a Committee of Congress that the American way of life is in greater jeopardy from the Cold War than it would be from a hot one. An open war—so he is reported as saying—America could win, but 'I do not know if we will win this Cold War or not'. I quote *The Times* of June 27, 1958. Mr Krushchev, on the other hand, in a letter to me, said:

'However much our opponents may slander us, the Socialist countries will not disappear because of that, and Communism, the most progressive and humanist teaching, will not cease to exist.

'How many attempts there have been to destroy Communism by force of arms! . . .

'I think that if imperialism unleashes a new world war, it will perish in it. The peoples will not want to put up with a system which cannot exist without wars, without the annihilation of millions of people, to enrich a handful of monopolists.'

I have no doubt that both Mr Dulles and Mr Krushchev have many followers who devoutly believe that a nuclear war would end in establishing the sort of world that they think good. In this chapter, I wish to give reasons for thinking this belief on either side completely mistaken. It is a dangerous belief both because it makes war more likely and because it is an obstacle to rational conciliation.

There are various possibilities as to how a nuclear war might begin. It might begin with a surprise attack from either side, but it might, also, grow out of an originally non-nuclear war. The United States Government has stated with great emphasis that it will never initiate a nuclear war, but this statement is subject to a qualification. Both Britain and the United States have said that, if Russia makes a non-nuclear attack upon any NATO country, the West will retaliate with nuclear weapons. It would seem to follow that Russia would have no motive for initially abstaining from nuclear weapons and that any war between East and West would almost necessarily be nuclear from the first.

It is obvious that the side which strikes first will gain great advantages from having the initiative. But, on the Western side, and presumably also on that of Russia, great pains have been taken to insure that a surprise attack shall not be decisive and shall not make retaliation impossible. I think we must, therefore, assume that the full potentialities of nuclear devastation will be developed against East and West equally.

How complete the devastation would be is a matter of controversy. Some optimists, who are afraid that their side may shirk the battle, maintain that not more than 30 per cent of mankind would perish, and such a loss they would regard with equanimity. But I think the pronouncements of those who have had the skill and the opportunity to make reasonable estimates lead to a very much more pessimistic conclusion. It must, however, be emphasized that there can be no certainty in this matter until after the event.

Let us begin by a statement by General Gavin, who was, at the time that he made the statement, Chief of Army Research and Development in the United States. He was giving testimony before the Symington Senate Committee. He was asked:

'If we got into a nuclear war and our strategic air force made an assault in force against Russia with nuclear weapons so that the weapons exploded in a way where the prevailing winds would carry them south-east over Russia, what would be the effect in the way of death?'

General Gavin replied:

'Current planning estimates run on the order of several hundred million deaths. That would be either way depending on which way the wind blew. If the wind blew to the south-east they would be mostly in the USSR, although they would extend into the Japanese and perhaps down into the Philippine area. If the wind blew the other way they would extend well back into Western Europe.'

This answer was disliked by the authorities, though they did not question its accuracy. There is every reason to believe that he was expressing the opinions of the United States authorities although they did not wish these opinions to be published at that moment.

More authoritative than General Gavin's statement is an estimate of probable casualties in the United States made by the Federal Civil Defence Administration. (Presumably similar estimates have been made and been similarly accepted in Russia.) This statement considers what would be likely to happen if nuclear weapons having a combined yield of 2,500 megatons were dropped on the United States. Taking the population as that of 1950 —namely, 151 million—they estimate that, on the first day, 36 million would be dead and 57 million injured, and that by the sixtieth day there would be 72 million dead and 21 million injured, leaving 58 million uninjured. Mr Dulles's own Government made this estimate, and we must therefore suppose that he would regard such an outcome as constituting a victory providing the number of the Russian dead were even larger. The above figures, being based on the population of 1950, must all be increased in the same proportion to be applicable to the present increased population.

The bare figures, however, fail to give a picture of what the state of affairs would be. In the first place, many of those listed as uninjured would, inevitably, suffer from fall-out in moving from place to place. In the second place, there could be no adequate medical care of the injured since most medical supplies and hospitals would be destroyed and a very large number of medical men and nurses would be dead. In the third place, since com-

munications and water supplies would almost certainly
be disrupted, it would be almost impossible to feed the
surviving populations of large cities. In the fourth place,
since drains and sewers would be largely destroyed, there
would probably be severe epidemics. Furthermore, it is
impossible to be sure that in such an appalling situation
any kind of social cohesion would survive. For all these
reasons, one must expect the actual number of dead to
be considerably larger than the above figure of 72 million.

All the disasters that we have been considering are to
result from one single day's bombing, and there is every
reason to expect that, in the course of a nuclear war,
there will be a number of such days. The National
Planning Association's Report, to which I alluded in my
last chapter, goes on to point out that,

'In addition to the figure which the FCDA has been able
to calculate for the radioactive deaths which might be
expected within two months of the hostilities, there will
be an undetermined number of further casualties during
the following fifty years, caused by genetic effects, tumor
induction, and the like. It is likely that in the countries
in which the bomb explosions occur, these delayed
casualties will equal the immediate ones. During these
following fifty years, the remainder of the world would
probably suffer some 10 million additional deaths as a
result of the induction of tumors and genetic effects from
the world-wide fallout. It is striking that the damage to
neutral countries may be as high as 5 to 10 per cent of
that suffered by the belligerents.'

All this, there is every reason to believe, would result

from one day's bombing of the United States by the Soviet Union. Other days would increase the casualties in the United States. Western Europe, including Britain, would probably suffer more than the United States owing to the greater density of population. The survivors, starving, debilitated, and incapable of giving birth to healthy children, would, I suppose, be expected to find consolation in the equal plight of the Russians. Do Mr Dulles and Mr Krushchev know all this? And do they consider that it would constitute victory? Or have they not taken the trouble to acquaint themselves with the probable consequences?

The amount of damage that will ultimately be caused to the survivors by fall-out is quite impossible to estimate. Although the damage from fall-out will, at first, be much greater in the neighbourhood of the places where bombs are dropped, it will, after a time, be distributed fairly evenly throughout the world. This is known from the effects of test explosions which have produced, even at great distances from all tests, serious quantities of the most deleterious substances, namely, Strontium 90, Caesium 137, and Carbon 14. There has been much talk in America of 'clean' bombs, which will have less of Strontium 90 and Caesium 137, but not of Carbon 14 which decays very slowly, having a half-life of 8,070 years, and will continue for thousands of years to have disastrous genetic effects. The tests that have already taken place are producing evils of which the magnitude is as yet uncertain. Dr Pauling (*No More War*, page 75) estimates that, if tests continue at the present rate, each year of testing will cause the birth of 230,000 seriously defective children and 420,000 embryonic and neo-natal deaths.

The so-called 'clean' bombs would therefore, even if employed, eliminate only a part of the fall-out damage, and I see no reason to expect that they would be employed. Dr Libby, who champions them, maintains that he does so from humanitarian motives. I asked him whether the Russians should be informed of American research into the possibility of 'clean' bombs, but he replied indignantly that that would be illegal. It would seem to follow that the humanitarian feelings which he has towards Russians do not extend to his compatriots. This, of course, cannot be the case, and, in fact, the talk of 'clean' bombs has little substance.

The picture drawn by the Federal Civil Defence Administration is sufficiently dreadful, but it must be remembered that, as Mr Charles Wilson, Secretary of Defence, informed a Senate Committee, 'our capability of inflicting this devastation is not static. It is improving and will continue to improve.' He was speaking of the capacity of the United States, but one must assume that the same is true of Russia. With every year that passes, the disasters to be expected from a nuclear war increase. When, as is hoped, the moon, and perhaps Mars and Venus, can be utilized as launching sites, there will be a sudden increase in the devastation to be expected. And although we now think H-bombs very terrible, there was a time, only thirteen years ago, when we shuddered at A-bombs. Nobel thought dynamite so destructive that it would put an end to war. Before long, if there is no change of policy, we shall look back to the happy, comfortable days of the H-bombs and wonder how anybody could have feared such trivial weapons. There is no conclusion possible in this march towards insane death except

to turn right round and march, instead, towards sanity
and life. Our present courses lead inevitably, sooner or
later, to the extinction of the human species. We are not
doomed to persist in the race towards disaster. Human
volitions have caused it, and human volitions can arrest it.

CHAPTER III

Methods of Settling Disputes in the Nuclear Age

I shall assume the following three propositions conceded:

(1) A large-scale nuclear war would be an utter disaster, not only to the belligerents, but to mankind, and would achieve no result that any sane man could desire.

(2) When a small war occurs, there is a considerable risk that it may turn into a great war; and in the course of many small wars the risk would ultimately become almost a certainty.

(3) If all existing nuclear weapons had been destroyed and there were an agreement that no new ones should be manufactured, any serious war would, nevertheless, become a nuclear war as soon as the belligerents had time to manufacture the forbidden weapons.

From these three theses, it follows that, if we are to escape unimaginable catastrophes, we must find a way of avoiding all wars, whether great or small and whether intentionally nuclear or not.

I think that, in a more or less undecided fashion, this conclusion is admitted by most of those who have studied the subject. But statesmen, both in the East and the West,

have not arrived at any possible programme for imple-
menting the prevention of war. Since the nuclear stalemate became apparent, the Governments of East and
West have adopted the policy which Mr. Dulles calls
'brinkmanship'. This is a policy adapted from a sport
which, I am told, is practised by some youthful degen-
erates. This sport is called 'Chicken!' It is played by
choosing a long straight road with a white line down
the middle and starting two very fast cars towards each
other from opposite ends. Each car is expected to keep
the wheels of one side on the white line. As they approach
each other, mutual destruction becomes more and more
imminent. If one of them swerves from the white line
before the other, the other, as he passes, shouts 'Chicken!',
and the one who has swerved becomes an object of con-
tempt. As played by irresponsible boys, this game is
considered decadent and immoral, though only the lives
of the players are risked. But when the game is played
by eminent statesmen, who risk not only their own lives
but those of many hundreds of millions of human beings,
it is thought on both sides that the statesmen on one side
are displaying a high degree of wisdom and courage, and
only the statesmen on the other side are reprehensible.
This, of course, is absurd. Both are to blame for playing
such an incredibly dangerous game. The game may be
played without misfortune a few times, but sooner or later
it will come to be felt that loss of face is more dreadful
than nuclear annihilation. The moment will come when
neither side can face the derisive cry of 'Chicken!' from
the other side. When that moment is come, the statesmen
of both sides will plunge the world into destruction.

Practical politicians may admit all this, but they argue

that there is no alternative. If one side is unwilling to risk global war, while the other side is willing to risk it, the side which is willing to run the risk will be victorious in all negotiations and will ultimately reduce the other side to complete impotence. 'Perhaps'—so the practical politician will argue—'it might be ideally wise for the sane party to yield to the insane party in view of the dreadful nature of the alternative, but, whether wise or not, no proud nation will long acquiesce in such an ignominious rôle. We are, therefore, faced, quite inevitably, with the choice between brinkmanship and surrender.'

This view has governed policy on both sides in recent years. I cannot admit that brinkmanship and surrender are the only alternatives. What the situation requires is a quite different line of conduct, no longer governed by the motives of the contest for power, but by motives appealing to the common welfare and the common interests of the rival parties. What needs to be done is, first of all, psychological. There must be a change oɪ mood and a change of aim, and this must occur on both sides if it is to achieve its purpose. Possibly the initiative, in so far as it is governmental, may have to come from uncommitted nations; but the general attitude to be desired is one which, in the committed nations of East and West, will have to be first advocated by individuals and groups capable of commanding respect.

The argument to be addressed to East and West alike will have to be something on the following lines. Each side has vital interests which it is not prepared to sacrifice. Neither side can defeat the other except by defeating itself at the same time. The interests in which the two sides conflict are immeasurably less important than those in

31

which they are at one. The first and most important of their common interests is survival. This has become a *common* interest owing to the nature of nuclear weapons.

It might be possible for Americans, or some of them, to desire a world containing no Russians; and it might be possible for Russians, or some of them, to desire a world containing no Americans; but neither Americans nor Russians would desire a world in which both nations had been wiped out. Since it must be assumed that a war between Russia and America would exterminate both, the two countries have a common interest in the preservation of peace. Their common survival should, therefore, be the supreme aim of policy on both sides.

A second motive for agreement is the need to escape from the burdens of the arms race. If present policies continue, this burden will grow greater and greater as time goes on. More and more expensive weapons will be invented, more and more labour will be diverted from the production of consumable commodities to the production of lethal weapons. Before very long, the population in each group will be reduced to subsistence level. New inventions, which in other circumstances might be beneficent, will no longer be so, since every increase in productivity will release more labour for warlike purposes. If one side rebels sooner than the other against the burden of this insanity, it will incur a risk of defeat and, in the bitter atmosphere produced by the dreadful danger, this risk will appear one to be avoided at almost any sacrifice.

It is not only prevention of evils, but the securing of immense goods, that can result from a cessation of tension between the two groups. Scientific technique has become capable of raising the standard of life in every part of the world, and more especially, in the poorer parts. There is no reason except human folly for the perpetuation of a lower standard of life in Asia and Africa than that which now prevails in America. But if the arms race continues, the standard of life in America must gradually decline towards the level now prevailing in the poorest parts of the world, and, instead of the universal material well-being which has become technically possible, we shall have a universal poverty as dire as mutual hatreds can cause rival nations to endure.

Nor is it only in material ways that the present hostility of East and West is harmful. It is even more harmful in the sphere of morality and emotion. We have been told on the highest governmental authority that, if Britain became involved in a nuclear war, no serious attempt would be made to defend the civilian population, but those in charge of missiles and bombs to be fired against Russia would be kept alive a little longer than the civilians and could in their last moments cause some hundreds of millions of deaths in Russia. These last survivors would die knowing that their own nation no longer existed, but enjoying (or so one must suppose) the sweet thought of a useless revenge. I am not saying this as a special criticism of British policy. A very similar policy is advocated throughout the two hostile groups. Even religion is often enlisted in its support, and many people sincerely though mistakenly believe that it can be justified by idealistic motives. The mentality which makes such an outlook possible, however sincere it may be, is morally dreadful and poisons all wholesome thought and feeling in those who allow themselves to be dominated by it.

For all these reasons, not only idealistic motives, but

the plainest and most insistent motives of self-interest make it imperative that East and West should no longer seek to settle their differences by war or the threat of war. If East and West, alike, can admit the force of the very plain and simple arguments in favour of this conclusion, it will no longer seem impossible to find other methods by which agreements as to disputed matters can be reached. Hitherto, agreements have been difficult because they were not genuinely desired by either side unless they constituted diplomatic victories. But, if it comes to be realized by both sides that it is more important to reach agreements than to win diplomatic victories, it will soon be found that impartial agreements are not nearly so difficult as was thought.

It should be made clear by those who advocate the point of view that I have been trying to recommend that it is a view put forward, not in the special interests of the West or in the special interests of the East, and that it does not aim at giving to either side any advantage not balanced by an equal advantage to the other side. The essential points which both sides must realize are that the continuation of conflict is disastrous to both, and that the gain to both to be derived from concord is one of quite immeasurable magnitude.

CHAPTER IV

Programme of Steps towards Peace

Those who realize the peril involved in the possibility of nuclear weapons have a very grave responsibility. The dangers are new, and the kind of thinking that they demand is also new. If mankind is to survive in the nuclear age, it can only be by the prevention of large-scale wars. This is a difficult end to achieve. And if it is to be achieved in spite of the prejudices and mental habits of populations and politicians, it will have to be approached by stages and with comprehension of opposing points of view.

The problem is not merely to discover measures which, if adopted, would prevent war, but to discover measures which, in addition to this merit, are also such as Governments and public opinion, both in the East and in the West, can be induced to support. Measures which are to have both these merits must be such as to give no net advantage to either side and to secure to the various nations involved the preservation of those interests which they consider completely vital.

In the approach towards a stable peace, there will have to be a number of stages, of which the earlier ones will be comparatively easy. The first step is to persuade the Governments of East and West that their aims cannot be

secured by a large-scale war. The second step is to persuade the Governments of West and East that their
opposite numbers are convinced of this obvious truth. It
has been customary in recent years for each side to suspect
the other of insincerity in negotiations, and it cannot be
said that either side has been without grounds for this
suspicion. If negotiations are to prove fruitful, there must
not only, in fact, be sincerity on each side, but there must
also be belief in the sincerity of the other side. The word
'sincerity', however, demands some definition. It is not
to be supposed that diplomats on either side will suddenly
become indifferent to the interests of the Powers that they
represent. The kind of sincerity that is required is something different. It consists in the desire to reach agreement,
as opposed to the desire to find proposals which the other
side will reject in spite of suffering propaganda disadvan-
tage by doing so. If negotiations are sincere in the sense
required, it will have to be acknowledged in advance that
they must not be expected to involve any net loss to either
party. If each side has genuinely abandoned war as an
instrument of policy, it will be obvious that any agreements reached by negotiation must have the character
of not altering the balance of power. This does not involve
renunciation by either side of the belief that a change
in the balance of power might be desirable. On this
matter, each party may retain its beliefs, but it will have
to alter the methods by which their success is to be
furthered. The methods will have to be those that are
adopted in the party politics of democratic countries, that
is to say they will have to be methods of peaceful persuasion and not of armed force.

One step, which has already, in part, been taken, is the

abandonment of mutual vituperation. The West thinks
the Kremlin wicked, and the East thinks Wall Street
wicked. Neither side, in the past, showed any reticence
in the expression of these mutual detestations, and there
is still room for considerable improvement, but if negotiations are to be fruitful, a certain degree of mutual courtesy
is indispensable. Apart from this consideration, belief in
the wickedness of possible enemies is apt to become
exaggerated and melodramatic. It would be well to
remember that men are not merely political and that,
outside the political sphere, there is little important
difference between East and West as regards purely
human hopes and fears and joys and sufferings. The
propaganda machine on both sides should turn from
promoting hate to promoting awareness of common
humanity. This, I repeat, is already being achieved in
some measure but in nothing like the degree that is to
be desired.

The first matter upon which we may hope for governmental agreement is the abolition of nuclear tests. This
is within the sphere of immediate practical politics.
Although it is only a first step, it is capable of having
considerable importance. In the first place, it puts an end,
for the time being, to the diffusion of man-made poisons
which must have already caused an unknown amount of
cancer and genetic damage and will cause more and more
of such damage as long as the tests continue. Much more
important than this consideration, is the fact that a general
agreement to suspend tests will prevent the spread of
nuclear weapons to Powers which at present do not
possess them. This spread is imminent, and if it takes
place it will very greatly increase the danger of nuclear

war. There is another reason for welcoming an agreement to abandon tests: namely, that any agreement between East and West about anything is to the good. The long wrangles that have disgraced disarmament conferences have brought the friends of peace to the verge of despair, and it will be a source of hope if it is proved that on this point agreement is possible.

I think the next step should be a solemn joint declaration by the United States and the USSR to the effect that they will seek to settle their differences otherwise than by war or the threat of war, and that, to implement this declaration, they should appoint a permanent joint body to seek measures tending towards peace and not altering the existing balance of power. I am not suggesting that such a body should be entrusted with decisive power, at any rate until its procedures had been tested in practice. What I am suggesting is that it should be invited to study every dispute that might arise and to suggest such settlement as each side might be willing to accept. I do not think that definitive conclusions could be quickly reached, since any global agreement would be favourable to one side in some parts of the world and to the other in other parts, so that it would have to be treated as an indivisible whole and not divided into separate matters.

The questions that have to be decided are of two sorts, though the two cannot be rigidly separated. There are questions of disarmament and there are territorial questions. As to the latter, it should be agreed that, during negotiations, the *status quo* should be maintained; but as to the former, something more immediate is necessary.

What gives urgency to disarmament questions is the very real risk of unintended war. The doctrine of instant retaliation, proclaimed by the West and presumably adopted also by the East, is one which exposes the world to an appalling risk not sufficiently acknowledged by statesmen or sufficiently realized by the public. Each side proclaims that it will never make an unprovoked nuclear attack, but it does not feel certain that the other side will show equal virtue. It is known that some accident may be misinterpreted as a nuclear attack and that retaliation may occur before the mistake is discovered. The danger will be very much increased if many Powers have nuclear weapons. An attack by one of the minor Powers would almost certainly be thought to be an attack by one of the major Powers and would, therefore, precipitate a major war within an hour or two. It is of the utmost urgency that means should be found of averting such dangers. No measures of conciliation can give any degree of security while each side remains in readiness to repel any supposed attack by instant full-scale retaliation.

CHAPTER V

New Outlook Needed before Negotiations

It is not the purpose of this chapter to suggest specific measures for the diminution of the likelihood of nuclear war. For the present, I will consider only the general outlook which should prevail on both sides if negotiations are to have a chance of success. The first thing necessary is a new assessment of national interests in all the powerful countries of the world. The measures which should be suggested with a view to the preservation of peace ought all to be such as to further the national interests of all the countries concerned. The new assessment that is called for consists only in an acknowledgement of facts, not in a change of aims. It is for this reason that an appeal to Governments may hope to succeed, since neither side is asked to renounce anything that is practicable.

Powerful countries hitherto have had two kinds of purposes in their policy: on the one hand, they have sought the prosperity of their own countries; on the other hand, they have sought dominion, political, economic or ideological, over other countries. This second aim has usually been pursued by means of war. What is new in the present situation is that the pursuit of foreign dominion by means of war is much less possible than it used to be. It is still as possible as it ever was for Governments to promote the internal prosperity of their countries, but foreign dominion, except where it already exists, is no longer a possible road to the prosperity of an imperialistic country. A statesman who aims at making his own country safe and prosperous can now only achieve his aim by making all powerful countries safe and prosperous. This is not due to any new morality. It is due solely to the potentialities of scientific warfare. You may, if you are a Russian, consider that it would be a good thing if all the world were Communist. You may, if you are an American or a Western European, consider that it would be a good thing if all the world adopted the political and economic system of your own country. Nobody should be asked to renounce either of these opinions; but what must be renounced is the belief that either can be achieved through a world war.

This is something definitely new in human history. In the conflicts between Christianity and Islam, it was war that decided which countries should be Christian and which Mohammedan. In the conflicts between Protestants and Catholics, it was again military success and failure that decided the issue. America, North and South, is Christian because European arms were more effective than those of Red Indians. This long history has become so deeply embedded in the outlook of both statesmen and ordinary men that it is extremely hard to think in the new terms required in the modern world. Prominent authorities in America, Britain, Russia and China have in quite recent times expressed their belief that the ideology which they favour could be rendered world-wide by a nuclear war. It is impossible to know whether such pronouncements are wholly sincere or whether they are only part of a game of bluff. Whichever they may be, they are exceedingly dangerous. If they are only bluff, there is a danger that the bluff may be called.

It is impossible to know with any precision what the outcome of a nuclear war would be. Some think that half the population of the world would survive, some think only a quarter, and some think none. It is not necessary, in considering policy, to decide among such possibilities. What is quite certain is that the world which would emerge from a nuclear war would not be such as is desired by either Moscow or Washington. On the most favourable hypothesis, it would consist of destitute populations, maddened by hunger, debilitated by disease, deprived of the support of modern industry and means of transport, incapable of supporting educational institutions, and rapidly sinking to the level of ignorant savages. This, I repeat, is the most optimistic forecast which is in any degree plausible. It is not a forecast that can be welcome to the advocates of any present-day ideology, or to any humane person, or even to anybody possessed of the rudiments of sanity. It is on this kind of ground that the national interests of different States, however they may conflict on minor issues, are all identical on one point: that nuclear war must be prevented.

What is required is not any sacrifice of national interests, but only a more just appraisal of what those interests involve. Suppose that you are a patriotic Russian, or a patriotic Briton, or a patriotic American, if you think in old-fashioned terms, you will have purposes of two kinds: on the one hand, you will seek such internal measures as are likely to promote the welfare of your own citizens; on the other hand, you will seek means of promoting your nation's welfare at the expense of the welfare of other nations. This latter part of your aims has hitherto been pursued mainly by means of war. It cannot now be pursued by this means. I do not say that it cannot be pursued *at all*: Russia profits by the uranium of Czechoslovakia, and Britain profits by the oil of the Middle East, but both these situations arose before the present nuclear deadlock. Further extensions of the domination of either the Eastern or the Western bloc, if they are such as would be resisted by war, are no longer possible.

The situation in its schematic simplicity is this: although a nuclear war would be disastrous to everybody, there are certain issues for which people would fight even if it were clear that fighting would do no good. A way must therefore be found of avoiding such issues. And this will only be possible if each side, quite genuinely and quite sincerely, abandons the hope of success by means of war. Let us try to give some concrete substance to this rather abstract statement. Some prominent Russians believe, or profess to believe, that the ordinary citizen of the United States groans under the tyranny of Wall Street and would welcome the opportunity to enjoy such 'freedom' as is offered by the Kremlin. Many people in the United States believe, or profess to believe, that the Soviet Government is hated in Russia and that a majority of Russians would welcome the opportunity of rebelling against it. Such beliefs on either side must not be allowed to influence policy, since, on each side, the opposing belief will, if necessary, be resisted by force. It may be that the future belongs to Communism, it may be that it belongs to the American way of life, it may be that it belongs to neither. Those who favour either should be free to spread their belief by peaceful propaganda. Christian missionaries, no doubt, hope that in time all the world will be Christian, but most of them no longer appeal to armed force to support their missionary efforts. In like manner, adherents of the Eastern system or of the Western system should be unhampered in their missionary efforts so long as they sincerely renounce world-conquest by military methods. At present, the East fears the West, and the West fears the East, in each case because, not wholly without reason, each side fears that the other aims at world-conquest by arms. Since modern weapons have made this aim unattainable, it is time that it was abandoned on both sides, and abandoned with such sincerity as would leave each side in no doubt that the other had abandoned it.

On this question of sincerity the initial difficulties are very great. Ever since 1945 they have rendered all negotiations abortive. If mutual trust is to be gradually generated, it will have to be by such measures on both sides as could only be prompted by a genuine desire for peace without victory for either side. Perhaps the first and most convincing proof of sincerity that could be given would be the abandonment of secrecy by both sides. If each side allowed all its armaments to be inspected by the other side, that would afford a fairly convincing proof that war was not surreptitiously intended. Another fairly convincing measure, which might offer less difficulty, would be an agreement to invite neutrals as arbitrators in difficult disputes. These, however, are only preliminary suggestions of which I shall have more to say in subsequent chapters.

There is one very simple matter in which improvement is possible without any negotiations or any formal agreements. The authorities on both sides should revert to the official courtesy which used to be observed between Governments, and should abstain from publicly imputing tortuous motives to all moves that appear prima facie to be conciliatory. The ascription of superior morality to one's own side, which has been for many years habitual both in the East and in the West, is so irritating to negotiators as to make it humanly very difficult to refrain from ruinous retorts. Among the courtesies of debate should be included a cessation of threats of attack and of the suggestion that the other side is contemplating attack or likely to indulge in it. The harm done by threats consists not only in the exacerbating of tempers, but in the constant revival and increase of mutual fears both in the authorities and in the population. This is a simple and elementary matter, but I believe that, if adopted by the official representatives of East and West, it would enormously facilitate the approach to fruitful agreements.

CHAPTER VI

Disarmament

There are many who consider that the problem of agreed disarmament or reduction of armaments is the most important in the field of international relations and the one to be first dealt with. I do not share this view. Needless to say, I consider agreed reduction of armaments very important and I favour the complete prohibition of all nuclear weapons, whether strategic or tactical. I see, however, two objections to treating this as the central and primary problem: First, as the experience of the last thirteen years has shown, disarmament conferences cannot reach agreements until the relations of East and West become less strained than they have been; second, the long-run problem of saving mankind from nuclear extinction will only be postponed, not solved, by agreements to renounce nuclear weapons. Such agreements will not, of themselves, prevent war, and, if a serious war should break out, neither side would consider itself bound by former agreements, and each side would, in all likelihood, set to work to manufacture new H-bombs as quickly as possible. These two considerations belong to different ends of the long road towards secure peace. The first prevents nations from starting along the road; the second shows a possibility of their being deflected after travelling a long way towards the goal. For these reasons, I should regard agreed disarmament as a palliative rather than a solution.

Nevertheless, the importance of any agreed measure of disarmament would be very great indeed. Perhaps its first and greatest importance would consist in the proof that negotiations between East and West can bear fruit in measures that all sane men must welcome.

The second gain would be a diminution of the risk of unintended war. The present readiness for instant retaliation makes it possible for some wholly accidental misfortune, such as a meteor exploding an H-bomb, to be mistaken for enemy action. Since it is assumed, probably rightly, that a Great Power, if embarked upon nuclear war, would begin by destroying the seat of government of the enemy, it is inferred that subordinate commanders must not wait for orders from headquarters but must carry out plans previously arranged to meet the emergency. Many things more probable than collision with a meteor might initiate a war that no Great Power had intended. One such cause would be a mechanical defect in radar. Another would be a sudden nervous breakdown of some important officer as a result of the stress caused by appalling responsibility. A third, and even more likely source of danger, will arise when many countries have nuclear weapons. It will then be possible for a small country with an irresponsible, chauvinistic Government, to make a nuclear attack which would be interpreted as coming from a major Power and would, therefore, lead to world war before the error was discovered. For such reasons, the present state of the world, and still more the state which will exist when, as now seems nearly certain, a great many States possess H-bombs, involves quite appalling dangers which could be very greatly lessened by disarmament agreements.

A third reason for desiring a reduction of armaments is economy. The importance of this reason is likely to increase and become more evident during the next few years. Western Governments, faced by fear of mounting expenditure, have recently adopted the view that nuclear weapons almost alone could afford adequate defence. This view is being increasingly challenged by experts on the ground that the United States could suffer unendurably from a nuclear attack and would, therefore, be very unwilling to provoke a nuclear war. It follows that, if the West is to be capable of resisting the East without disaster, it must be able to conduct non-nuclear wars, although the ability to do so involves enormously increased expenditure. Apart from this somewhat technical consideration, one must assume that, so long as the arms race continues and remains a matter of life and death to both sides, new inventions will constantly increase military expenditure until both sides are reduced to subsistence level. The only escape will be when both sides realize that it is more profitable to keep one's own citizens prosperous than to be able to kill those of other countries.

The fourth gain which may be secured by disarmament agreements is that they may show the necessity of deciding disputes by arbitration or by some international tribunal, rather than by war or the threat of war. This is an almost inevitable logical consequence of any such agreement. Decision by war implies the use of the whole of a nation's strength if that is necessary for victory. A disarmament agreement on the other hand, so long as it is respected, implies that the Government is not using its whole strength in preparation for war. This leads inevitably to the conclusion that new methods of settling disputes must be sought.

Granted that a reduction of armaments is desirable, we are faced at once by formidable problems. After studying the proceedings of disarmament conferences, it is almost impossible not to be lost in a morass of technicalities, with arguments this way and that and well-founded objections that are met by equally well-founded retorts. So long as the East-West tension remains what it has been, I do not think that we are likely to escape from this morass. Suppose the East offers to agree to the abolition of all nuclear weapons. The West at once retorts that the superior man-power of the East would give it an unfair advantage unless conventional armaments were reduced at the same time. Suppose this admitted. The next question that arises is: To what figure should the conventional armaments of East and West be reduced? Suppose this agreed, there arises a third and most difficult question: What endurable measures of inspection will insure that an agreement is being loyally carried out? Hitherto it has been found that such questions could be prolonged *ad infinitum* and that negotiators could continue throughout many years to advocate disarmament without incurring the risk of bringing it about. If disarmament negotiations are to succeed, it will only be when each side is persuaded that the other has abandoned the hope of conquest.

There is, it is true, one measure which is already within the sphere of practical politics, and that is the abolition of nuclear tests. To repeat what was said in Chapter IV. What makes this measure already possible is that scientists are agreed in believing that no serious nuclear test

can be concealed, given a system of inspection so little
onerous that neither side objects to it. Although the
stoppage of tests is only a small step, it will nevertheless
be very welcome if it takes place. It will be welcome, first,
because it will put an end to the increase of radio-active
substances in air and water and food which at present is
causing an increase of cancer and leuchaemia and genetic
damage of unknown magnitude. It will be welcome, in
the second place, because any agreement between East
and West is to the good and tends to diminish tension.
It will be welcome, in the third place, because it will
make it more difficult for new Powers to join the 'Nuclear
Club'. For these reasons, we must all ardently hope that
an agreement to abolish tests will be reached.

Apart from the absence of any genuine governmental
desire for disarmament, the greatest difficulties are connected with the question of inspection. On this subject
there is an admirable book: *Inspection for Disarmament*,
edited by Seymour Melman, and published by the
Columbia University Press, New York, in 1958. So far
as I am able to judge, the investigations contained in this
book are completely honest and aim solely at a just
estimate of facts and probabilities. Broadly speaking, the
conclusion reached in this book is that inspection could
prevent the manufacture of new nuclear weapons, but
that it probably could not prevent a dishonest Government
from concealing some part of the stocks existing at the
time when an agreement was concluded. There is a
valuable account of the devices by which the German
Government, after the First World War, concealed the
armaments which it created in defiance of the Treaty of
Versailles. In this case, the acquiescence of the German

Government in the disarmament clauses of that Treaty was not voluntary, but was only a reluctant acquiescence in the consequences of defeat. I think we may infer that no disarmament agreement will be reliable unless all signatory States are sincerely convinced that it is to their own advantage, and not only to that of potential enemies. This re-enforces our earlier contention that disarmament must result from better relations between East and West, and cannot, by itself, be a cause of such better relations.

Given a genuine desire for peace on both sides, it should be possible, without undue delay, to agree that no new nuclear weapons should be manufactured. This is a measure which could be enforced by inspection without great difficulty. Aerial inspection, especially, would make the concealment of large plants almost impossible, even in the remotest regions of Siberia or Alaska. The destruction of existing stocks of H-bombs should follow, but offers greater difficulties, and, if it is to be carried out without altering the balance of power, it will have to be accompanied by a reduction of conventional forces. I doubt whether an agreement to this effect will be concluded until there is a genuine readiness on both sides to renounce war as an instrument of policy.

I should like, in conclusion, to say a few words about the increase of general well-being that would result if such measures of disarmament as we have been discussing were carried out. I put first among the gains to be expected the removal of that terrible load of fear which weighs at present upon all those who are aware of the dangers with which mankind is threatened. I believe that a great upsurge of joy would occur throughout the civilized world and that a great store of energies now turned to hate and destruction and futile rivalry would be diverted into creative channels, bringing happiness and prosperity to parts of the world which, throughout long ages, have been oppressed by poverty and excessive toil. I believe that the emotions of kindliness, generosity and sympathy, which are now kept within iron fetters by the fear of what enemies may do, would acquire a new life and a new force and a new empire over human behaviour. All this is possible. It needs only that men should permit themselves a life of freedom and hope from which they are now excluded by the domination of unnecessary fear.

CHAPTER VII

Steps towards Conciliation

Let us suppose a situation reached in which East and West alike are convinced that a nuclear war would be a disaster to all parties and that steps for the preservation of peace, if they were possible, would be supremely desirable. The obstacles to a peaceful policy are of various kinds. First, and most serious, is mutual fear and the suspicion of bad faith on the other side. The second obstacle is a fear of loss of face: neither side can bear to appear forced into concessions. A third difficulty, which is much emphasized but does not seem to me so grave as the other two, is the ideological dispute: a great many people on each side believe that the way of life for which their side stands is vastly better than the other and that nothing whatever must be done to give the other a chance of global success. I think that a policy of conciliation, if it is to win the support of the powerful, must take account of these difficulties and look for measures by which they may be minimized. I do not know whether such measures will be adopted and, if they are, I do not know what form they will take. In what follows, I will make suggestions as to a possible course that conciliation might take, but without wishing to insist upon just these measures if others having the same purpose were found more acceptable.

Perhaps the first step should be a solemn pronounce-
ment by the States in both blocs, and by any others that
cared to join in, to the effect that war could not serve
the purposes of any of the signatory Powers and that
measures for preventing it are, therefore, urgently to be
desired. This should be accompanied, or immediately
followed, by a stand-still agreement stipulating that,
during some specified period of time, no Power on either
side would attempt to alter the *status quo* or engage in any
provocative measure.

The next step should be the appointment of a Conciliation Committee, not intended to have any powers,
but to explore possible measures for the diminution of
tension. I think that if this Committee is to be effective
in its deliberations, it must be small. I should suggest:
two Americans, two Russians, one West European, one
Chinese, and two neutrals. The two neutrals might, perhaps with advantage, be one an Indian and the other
a Swede, since this would secure that, on the whole, one
should lean towards the East and the other towards the
West. It would be essential that the members of this
Committee should have the confidence of their respective
Governments since, otherwise, their recommendations
would not carry weight. During the period of their
deliberations, which could not be very brief, they should
have no other duties whatever. One of the difficulties in
the modern world is that all policy-makers are too busy
to be able to acquaint themselves with more than a small
proportion of the facts upon which policy ought to be
based. If the Conciliation Committee is not to suffer from
this defect, its members must be liberated both from
administrative burdens and from the daily pressure of

public opinion. It would be desirable for all the members of the Committee to meet together in daily contact, not only in a business way, but also socially. If, at some period of tension, the three Western members and the three Eastern members were to find themselves in such violent disagreement as to make discussion and social relations difficult, it should be the function of the two neutrals to smooth things over and bring both camps into a more tolerant mood. It should be understood from the first that agreement, rather than diplomatic victory, should be sought by each member of the Committee.

It would be an essential condition of success that discussions should be confidential and that nothing should be published without the unanimous consent of all the members. If this condition were not observed, it would be impossible for any member, during a debate, to make a tentative concession which the subsequent course of the debate might make inopportune. It would also make it very difficult for a member to avoid such opinions and such rhetoric as would win applause from the nation he represented. I think, however, that unanimous decisions, if any were reached, should be given the widest publicity in all the countries concerned.

Certain principles would have to be laid down as conditions for any acceptable agreements. The first and most absolute of these must be that conciliatory measures as a whole must give no net advantage to either side. The reason why this condition is so imperative is that there must be no temptation to either side to prefer war to the suggested measures of conciliation. I fear it is probable that any suggestion which genuinely satisfies this condition will appear to each side to be giving too much to the other. It will be the function of the two neutral members to satisfy themselves that there is a balance of concessions by the two sides, and, having satisfied themselves, to proceed to the persuasion of the other members.

The second principle that should govern the deliberations of the Committee is to seek ways of diminishing friction in difficult regions. What this demands, as a rule, is some decision which both sides agree to enforce and which will, therefore, be practically irrevocable. The friction that arises in various regions is fostered by uncertainty and by rivalries between East and West. If these were eliminated, most of the present dangers in such regions would disappear.

The third principle—which, however, should be subordinated to the other two—is that, wherever possible, the wishes of the inhabitants should be respected. For various reasons, this cannot be made an absolute principle. If, to take a fantastic example, there were a majority of Communists in Panama, one could not expect the United States to surrender the Canal to friends of Moscow. I will not give less fantastic examples for fear of rousing controversial passions.

I should hope that, after a suitable period of discussion, the Conciliation Committee would produce a draft agreement dealing with all the important points in which the interests of East and West are thought to conflict. I do not suggest that any Government should commit itself in advance to accepting any of the proposals of the Conciliation Committee, but I believe and hope that their proposals, when widely publicized, would form a nucleus about which sane opinion could quickly crystallize. Their proposals would have the merit of impartiality and of offering the best terms that any Government could reasonably expect. The mere fact of a suggested agreement, endorsed by representatives of East and West alike, would almost inevitably have a profound effect upon public opinion, and would give to the friends of peace a policy that could not be suspected of unduly favouring either side.

Many people will doubt whether such a Committee as I have been suggesting would be able to reach any kind of agreement. It will be said that the chasm between East and West is too wide to be bridged by discussion and that, even if the Committee reached agreements, the national Governments on each side would repudiate them as involving intolerable concessions. I do not think that this would be the case if the dangers of nuclear war had been adequately appreciated. When both sides realize that they are faced by a common danger, agreement is often found to be much easier than had been thought. I will give an illustration from an event which occurred a little more than half a century ago. Britain and Russia had hated and feared each other ever since the Crimean War, but, after over fifty years of mutual suspicion, they came to the conclusion that each had less to fear from the other than from Germany and, in the year 1907, they concluded an *entente* by which an end was put to all the divergencies between their policies. This happened through the common fear of Germany—a fear far less dreadful than the fear of nuclear warfare. It is profoundly unfortunate that the danger of nuclear warfare is regarded nationally rather than humanly. The East fears Western armaments; the West fears those of the East. In fact, the armaments of East and West alike threaten West and

57

East equally. This is obvious to anyone who has time to consider the matter and who is not obsessed by the nationalist ambitions of Foreign Offices. If it were apprehended by the statesmen of East and West alike, the differences at present dividing the two blocs would soon be found no more intractable than those that divided Britain and Russia before 1907. For these reasons I cannot despair of the success of such conciliatory deliberations as I have been suggesting.

CHAPTER VIII

Territorial Adjustments

The Conciliation Committee that I spoke of in the previous chapter will have as one of its most difficult tasks the suggestion for such territorial changes as may be considered necessary in the interests of peace. It cannot be known in advance what will be possible in this way, and what is to be said must be very tentative and liable to drastic changes when practical negotiations are undertaken. But, in spite of these uncertainties, it may be worth while to make a blue-print of what friends of peace might wish to see. The most important questions concerned may be divided into three heads: Europe, the Middle East, and the Far East.

(1) *Europe.* Europe is at present entirely dominated by the fear of war. In Western Europe there are United States forces and preparations for a nuclear attack on Russia. We are assured that the West would not initiate an attack, but that, if Russia attacked even with conventional arms, the West would retaliate with nuclear weapons. In Eastern Europe, on the other hand, Russia has established Communist Governments in a number of satellite States of which some, at least, contain a majority strongly opposed to Communism. The Govern-

ments which Russia has established in satellite States are kept in power by means of Russian troops. Europe is thus virtually partitioned between the United States in the West and Russia in the East. Before there can be any hope of stable peace, very radical measures must be adopted to put a neutral barrier between Russia and America and to restore independence of action to intermediate countries.

There is one very simple measure which would go a long way towards securing this result. It might be agreed that no sovereign State, whether in Eastern or Western Europe, should have any alien armed forces on its territory. This would entail very serious sacrifices both for America and for Russia. America has not, at present, the means of sending H-bombs from the United States to Russia, but can send them from any part of Western Europe, including Britain. The power of H-bomb attack upon Russia would be lost to America if no American armed forces were permitted in Europe. From the militarist point of view, this would be a very serious deprivation.

But Russia, also, would lose by such an agreement, and I think that her loss would be as great as America's. If there were no Russian armaments to be feared, Hungary and Eastern Germany certainly, and probably also Poland, would abandon Communism in favour of some kind of parliamentary Socialism. This, of course, could only happen if there were no serious reason to fear a Russian invasion. It would be necessary, therefore, not only that the countries of Europe should be freed from alien forces, but also that their immunity should be guaranteed. It would be desirable to neutralize all Central Europe from the Rhine to the Vistula, and to limit severely the armed forces permitted to the neutralized States. Russia, not unnaturally, is much afraid of German re-armament. In view of Russian experience during the two World Wars, this is certainly not surprising. On the other hand, Germany cannot be expected to acquiesce at all willingly in the partition between Eastern and Western Germany. There cannot be secure peace in Europe until Germany is reunited, and, if this is not to cause alarm to the Russians, it will have to be accompanied by an agreed limitation of German armaments.

There are two general principles that should be observed in any European settlement: the first is to lessen all possible causes of friction; and the second is to permit each country to decide for itself what political and economic system it may prefer. Except for a limitation of armaments, there should be no interference with the internal affairs of any sovereign State. If it preferred Communism, the West should not object; if it preferred parliamentary democracy, Russia should leave it free to do so.

I do not think that the removal of American forces from Western Europe can become practical politics except as a sequel to an enforceable agreement for the abolition of nuclear weapons. If there is no such agreement, America, in the absence of European centres of occupation, is not on an equality with Russia, and Western Europe, which depends upon American protection, can feel no security. It is for this sort of reason that territorial questions cannot be wholly separated from questions of disarmament, and that any conciliation that is proposed must embrace *all* problems involved between East and West.

(2) *The Middle East.* There are two very intractable problems connected with the Middle East: the one is oil, the other is Israel. As regards oil, Western Europe has allowed its economy to be deeply dependent upon the oil of the Middle East. In the cheerful days of British and French imperialism, this raised no great difficulty. The countries of the Middle East could be compelled by military power to consent to the exploitation of their resources by Western capitalist interests. But those days are past. Arab nationalism, encouraged by Russia, is in a position to insist upon independence and to demand of the West much higher terms than were formerly obtainable. Although this is unpleasant for the West, it need not be disastrous. The West will have to come to terms with Arab nationalism and will have to make such economic concessions as will cause Arab nations to be still willing to sell their oil to Western Europe. The West, and specially Britain and France, has made the mistake of showing hostility to the new forces in the Middle East to which the Russians have shown themselves friendly. If the need of oil is no longer to lead the West to support ancient evils, there will have to be a radical change of outlook in Britain and France. And if a *détente* between Russia and the West is to be genuine, there will have to be a measure of agreement as to the policy to be adopted towards the countries of the Middle East. The West will have to abandon its support of bad Governments, and Russia will have to restrain the desire to stir up trouble.

The question of Israel is one of the most difficult of those that have to be faced if conciliation is to be possible. The hatred of Israel in Arab countries is regrettable but understandable. Not only in Arab countries but throughout Asia, Israel is regarded as a piece of unwarrantable Western imperialism. The fact that the Jews originally came from Asia is forgotten; what is remembered is that, in the course of centuries, the great majority of them have become completely Westernized. The West, however, cannot abandon the State of Israel after deliberately creating it and guaranteeing its protection. I think the only thing that can be done is to fix unalterably the geographical frontiers of Israel and undertake that Russia and the West, jointly, shall prevent any aggression by or against the State of Israel. If there were no uncertainty, and if the Great Powers were united in the matter, Jews and Arabs would in time get used to each other and discover that mutual hatred serves no purpose.

(3) *The Far East.* The conquest of China by the Communists is the severest blow that the West has suffered since Lenin's Government became secure. It cannot be denied that the Chinese Communists have given evidence of militaristic imperialism. Their intervention in the Korean War was as unjustified as it was unfortunate, and their conquest of Tibet was the kind of thing which is severely condemned when done by a Western Power. It is a pity, however, that the West has allowed its hostility to these adventures to dominate policy to a disastrous extent. No reasonable man can expect the Communists to lose control of China except in a universal cataclysm in which everybody loses control of everything. The pretence in America and UNO that Chiang represents China is unworthy of sensible men. It must be part of any measure of conciliation to give to the Communist Government of China the position in UNO which is now accorded to Chiang. The present policy of defending

Chiang will have to be abandoned. As regards Formosa, the best that his friends can reasonably hope is that he should conclude an agreement with Communist China leaving him in possession of Formosa for his lifetime on condition that, at his death, it should be joined to the mainland.

The importance of Formosa to America, like that of Cyprus to Britain, is strategic and is bound up with preparedness for a nuclear war. If the danger of nuclear war can be averted, these two troublesome islands can be allowed to go their own way, unhelped and unhindered by the Powers which have been attempting to control them. It will be said that the West will lose face if it makes concessions to Communist China, but such loss of face, if it occurs, will be the penalty of having embarked upon a fruitless policy. However regrettable, it is not so regrettable as persistence in a course which can only lead to disaster.

China is potentially as powerful as Russia or the United States, and may well be actually as powerful within a few decades. The peace of the world cannot be secure if China is aggressive and imperialistic, which there is grave danger of China becoming. America and Europe (including Russia) have certain common interests to defend against possible aggression from the East. The best defence consists, not in armaments, but in wise forbearance and a genuine desire for world peace. Of this spirit the Chinese, so far, have had no evidence. It is time that we gave them some reason to think better of us than they have done since the Opium War.

CHAPTER IX

Approach to an International Authority

The great majority of those who have considered the conditions for secure peace are persuaded that the most important of these conditions is the creation of an International Authority with power to enforce its decisions. This, however, remains for the present a merely academic opinion: while the East-West tension retains anything like its present acuteness, neither side would submit to any International Authority unless it could dominate it. The question at issue is, at bottom, one of great simplicity: would you rather have a world in which both friends and foes survive, or a world in which both are extinct? Put in these abstract terms, most people would prefer the survival of their friends to the extinction of their foes. But when it is pointed out to them that this choice, if made in earnest, requires some very distasteful measures, they will refuse to admit the necessity of such measures and will persist in the course leading to universal death. In this chapter, I wish to suggest comparatively painless steps by which an International Authority could gradually come into existence. These steps will only be possible after the measures of conciliation considered in earlier chapters; but if these measures have been adopted, the further steps that I am about to suggest may be accepted as a natural and logical sequel.

The first thing that should be done is to confirm the advisory authority of the Conciliation Committee outlined in Chapter VII. This Committee, however, will only be effective in disputes between East and West. For other disputes, measures less *ad hoc* will be necessary.

The League of Nations and the United Nations were both intended by their creators to be the germ of an International Authority capable of preventing war. Both failed, but the United Nations is perhaps still capable of being so reformed as to fulfil its intended function. The reforms required are, however, very drastic, and at present some, at least, are quite outside the domain of practical politics.

There is one very vital measure which may perhaps be adopted within a few years, and that is the admission to UNO of all States that desire membership. As everybody knows, the most urgent case is that of Communist China. China is the most populous State in the world and may, within a few decades, become the most powerful. It is clear that a body intended to be international and impartial cannot fulfil its functions while such an important country is excluded. But China is only the most glaring example of exclusion. There can be no good reason for keeping out any country which is willing to undertake the obligations imposed by the United Nations Organization.

There is a difficulty which faces all federal organizations, namely, that some members of the federation are more powerful or more populous than others and that it therefore does not seem just that all should carry equal weight. This problem faced the framers of the American Constitution, and, as everybody knows, they adopted a compromise solution: In the Senate, all States are equal, but, in the House of Representatives, their weight is proportional to their population. Some arrangement will be necessary in the Constitution of the reformed United Nations if small States are not to have undue weight. The present arrangement, according to which all States count equally in the Assembly, but, in the Security Council, certain powerful States have a veto, is open to various objections which I shall consider presently. One possible solution—which, I admit, has its own difficulties —would be to divide the world into a number of subordinate Federations, each of which should be a member of the one World-wide Federation. These subordinate Federations should be framed in accordance with two principles: first, they should all be approximately equal in population so that there would be no serious injustice in counting each as one in the federation of Federations which would be the reconstituted UNO; the second principle should be that, as far as possible, each Federation should have internal interests outweighing those concerning its external relations. It should be generally understood, though not formally decreed, that, in general, each subordinate Federation should have autonomy in regard to its internal affairs and that only disputes between Federations should come before UNO. In this way, the interference of the International Authority in local affairs could be reduced to a minimum.

The Veto, which was adopted in 1945 when the United Nations was created, was a practical necessity at that time. Both the United States and the USSR were agreed on this point. There is no likelihood that the Veto will be abolished until such time as East and West have become much more conscious of their common interests than they now are. But so long as the Veto exists, UNO lacks an essential characteristic of any Government. It is of the essence of a Government that it can enforce decisions upon recalcitrant members of the State which it represents. What should we think of a national State in which any burglar could veto laws against theft? There was once a national State constituted in this manner. It was the State of Poland. The *liberum veto* which existed in that country reduced it to impotence and rendered it incapable of resisting partition among its powerful neighbours. Nevertheless, it was this example which was followed when UNO was created. Already at that time the divergent interests of East and West made such a course inevitable. But if there is ever to be an International Authority capable of preventing large-scale war, it will have to be an Authority in which the Veto does not exist, since, otherwise, it will be unable to settle any dispute in which either side is prepared to use the Veto.

There will need to be, as in any Federation, a well-defined Constitution deciding which powers are to be federal. It should be understood that these powers must be only such as are involved in the prevention of war. There must be no interference by the Federal Authority with religion or economic structure or the political system. If some nations prefer parliamentary democracy, and others prefer some form of dictatorship, they must be free to persist in their choice. They must be similarly free if some prefer Communism and others prefer Capitalism. I think they must also be free to impose such limits upon individual liberty as they may consider desirable. I do not think that the Federal Authority ought to impose freedom of the Press or any other freedom upon any subordinate State. I say this in spite of realizing the importance of such freedoms. I say it because only the prevention of war gives outside States a justification for interference.

We have, I am afraid, already travelled a long way into Utopian regions, but there is a last step even more Utopian that must be taken if world peace is to be secure. There must be an International Armed Force sufficiently powerful to be certain of victory over the armed forces of any nation or likely alliance of nations. In the absence of this condition, the decrees of the International Authority may not be enforceable and may easily sink to the level of empty pronouncements like the Kellogg Pact. The International Authority will have to be free to create such armed forces as it thinks necessary and to impose such taxation as they may require. It will also need a legal right to limit the armed forces of national States so as to prevent any serious threat to its authority.

All this, however utopian it may appear, is only a close parallel to what happened in national States as a result of the invention of gunpowder. In the Middle Ages throughout Western Europe powerful barons in their castles could defy the central Government. It was only when artillery became able to destroy castles that the central Government was able to control feudal barons. What gunpowder did in the late Middle Ages, nuclear weapons have to do in our time. I do not mean that they have to be actually employed. Gunpowder does not often have to be employed to enforce the authority of national Governments against internal criminals. And similarly the actual employment of nuclear weapons will not be necessary if no national State possesses them and only the International Authority has the means of manufacturing them.

If an International Armed Force is to be both effective and safe, it will have to fulfil certain conditions. It must not be composed of large contingents contributed by national States, since such contingents would be likely to retain their national loyalties and could not be relied upon to obey a decree which they disliked. It will be necessary that each battalion, each squadron, and each submarine should contain men of various different nations so that mutiny in some national interest would be impossible. So long as the divergence between East and West persists, it would be desirable that the Supreme Command should belong to a member of an uncommitted nation.

Whenever an international armed force is suggested, many people at once raise objections which are equally applicable to municipal police forces. They suggest that such an armed force might make a military revolution and establish a tyranny over the civil authorities. In theory this is possible in the case of national armed forces, and in the less settled parts of the world it sometimes occurs. But there are well-established methods, both in Communist and in non-Communist countries, by which, not only in Russia and in the United States, but even in Nazi Germany, the civil authorities have maintained their supremacy. I see no reason to doubt that these methods would be equally effective in the international sphere.

In any case, governmental and legal control over the relations between national States has become necessary to survival. I do not mean that it is necessary from one day to the next. The world may go on for some time with brinkmanship and, with luck, it may not go over the brink. But luck cannot be counted upon to continue indefinitely. Sooner or later, present policies, if persisted in, must lead to disaster. Submission to a Central Authority may be as distasteful as submission to the king was to mediaeval barons, but it is in the long run equally necessary. Although an International Authority is not yet practical politics, it must be the ultimate goal of all those who wish to preserve the world from the disasters of nuclear war.

I have spoken of some of the above measures as Utopian, and I think in the present political climate they must be so regarded. I think that a long and serious work in the way of conciliation and lessening of mutual fanaticism will be a necessary preliminary to the creation of a powerful international force. But there are those who consider the creation of such a force more quickly possible than I have supposed. And to my great satisfaction, I find that this view is influentially advocated in the British Conservative Party. The Conservative Political Centre has published a pamphlet by ten Conservative Members of Parliament entitled 'A World Security Authority?'. The measures advocated in this pamphlet are very similar to most of those outlined above. The authors of the pamphlet rely upon statements by the present British Prime Minister and by Mr Duncan Sandys, the Minister of Defence, supporting the view that World Government affords the only radical solution of the world's troubles. I hope the authors are right in their view as to what is practicable, but I am afraid that they will encounter very stubborn resistance in the two most powerful protagonists, namely, America and Russia. The world is faced with a race between reason and death. Advocates of death point out, with a lamentable degree of truth, that reason is a very feeble force in human affairs. So long as this is the case, hopes and fears must remain balanced in any forecast of the future.

CHAPTER X

Some Necessary Changes in Outlook

Some of the measures advocated in the preceding pages are such as will, in the present temper of the world, arouse vehement opposition both in the West and in the East. They are advocated as not improbable minimum conditions for a continued existence of *homo sapiens*. But certain widespread prejudices prevent clear thinking on the subject of international relations and make it difficult for intelligence to operate freely in this sphere. I wish in this chapter to deal with the most important of these obstacles and with the ways by which they can be overcome.

I. FANATICISM

There are many people in the West, and I suppose also in the East, who consider that the extermination of the human race would be preferable to the victory of the ideology that they dislike. They maintain that the evils inflicted by the Kremlin or by Wall Street, as the case may be, are so great that, in a world dominated by either, life would not be worth living and it would be a kindness to future generations to prevent them from being born. On this ground it is argued that, if nothing short of a nuclear war can prevent the victory of the other side, a nuclear war should be waged even should it involve a risk of universal death. I cannot but regard such a point of view as one exhibiting ferocious fanaticism. By a curious inconsistency, those in the West who take this point of view maintain that they are defending democracy, although they must be aware that a plebiscite of the world would give an overwhelming majority against them. And it is not only democracy, but also freedom that these fanatics consider themselves to be defending. I sometimes wonder how they would phrase their argument in a discussion (say) with an inhabitant of India. An Indian would be very likely to say that he considered both the Russian and the Western ideologies partly good and partly bad, but that the greater portion of what makes up the lives of most human beings is independent of ideologies and can exist under either system. Our fanatic would have to tell him that such a point of view is base—in fact, so base as to be worthy of the death penalty. I do not think he would be able to persuade his Indian interlocutor that such punishment is deserved either in the name of democracy or in the name of freedom.

I think the argument with which we are concerned can, with profit, be considerably widened. The great majority of mankind, even in politically educated countries, are occupied throughout the greater part of their time with quite unpolitical matters. They are concerned to eat and sleep; they are concerned with love and family; they are concerned with success or failure in their work, and with the joy or pain of living, according to the state of their health. If you were to say to any ordinary person, seriously and as a practical issue: 'Would you rather live under a political and economic system different from your own or have all mankind die an agonizing death?' he would think you mad—and not without justification. Only a man who has lost his sense of human values through preoccupation with controversy can hesitate to answer this question as every sane man must answer it. Those who have been occupied in combating Communism or in combating Capitalism are likely to become obsessed by a belief that nothing else matters in comparison. In a life of dusty argument, they have lost all sight of everyday joys and sorrows.

But when it comes to preferring the extermination of mankind to the victory of an ideology which we dislike, there are other less general arguments to be considered. There have been many bad Governments and bad systems in the past. Genghis Khan, for example, was quite as bad as fanatical anti-Communists believe Stalin to have been. But his tyranny did not last for ever, and if his enemies had had the power to extinguish human life rather than submit to his brutalities, nobody in the present day would regret their not having exercised this power. Anybody who supposes that the tyranny of the Kremlin or the tyranny of Wall Street, as the case may be, would last for ever if for a moment it achieved world-victory, is being totally unhistorical and is showing himself an unbalanced victim of bugbears.

Issues that seemed to contemporaries as important as the issue of Communism or Capitalism seems to fanatics of the present day have repeatedly arisen in the past, and have been shown by the course of time to be not so tremendous as contemporaries suppose. There is a well-known passage in Gibbon in which he considers what would have happened if the Mohammedans had won the

Battle of Tours. To the Christians of that day, the issue appeared as momentous as the issue of our own time appeared to Senator McCarthy and to Stalin, but it may well be doubted whether the present-day world would be much different from what it is if the Mohammedans had been the victors and not the vanquished in that famous conflict.

So long as there are human beings, they will pursue their human purposes, partly good, partly bad. There will be systems of Government that inflict purposeless suffering, and there will be systems that make for human well-being. But if no human beings remain, the whole fabric of good and evil that men have gradually built up will be demolished. The pessimism of those who believe that under this or that system nothing good can ever emerge is to me incomprehensible.

Religious fanaticism has gradually decayed through experience of the futility of religious wars. Catholics and Protestants, Christians and Mohammedans have learnt to acquiesce in each other's existence, which was at one time thought quite impossible. But the newer controversies of our own time have caused many people to forget the tolerance which was slowly learned in the seventeenth and eighteenth centuries. When Locke wrote in favour of religious toleration, there were many who were outraged by his arguments; and there are many in the present day who are outraged when his arguments are applied to existing controversies. But the reasons which led to the success of his contentions had nothing to do with the particular nature of the controversies of his time. The reasons are valid now as they were valid then; and the arguments against toleration in our day are the same as the arguments of Loyola and Calvin at an earlier time. Many, both in the East and in the West, have forgotten the reasons which formerly produced tolerance. These reasons must be remembered if we are ever to find a solution for our troubles. Above all, we must remember that no one is infallible, not even ourselves, and that no dogma is so certain as to afford an excuse for widespread cruelty.

II. NATIONALISM

In any approach towards the creation of a World Authority, certain disruptive forces raise difficulties which at times seem almost insuperable. The opposition between Communism and Capitalism is the most notable obstacle to world unity at the present day; but there is another, namely nationalism, which would remain if Communism and Capitalism had learnt to tolerate each other. Nationalism in each nation consists partly of beliefs as to one's own nation's excellence, and partly of ethical maxims supposed to follow from these beliefs.

I shall be speaking mainly of the bad aspects of nationalism, but I wish to say emphatically that it has also its good aspects. It would not be a good thing if people all over the world were alike. Culturally, the differences between different nations give a desirable variety and are a stimulus in literature and art. It is only when nationalism leads to armed strife that it becomes a danger. It is wholly a good thing when a nation has independence in everything except violent hostility to other nations. If an International Authority is ever created, it will have to limit its interferences with national

States to matters likely to disturb international peace. If it does more than this, it becomes tyranny.

But, having said this, we must now turn our attention to the dangerous aspects of nationalism. Unlike Capitalism and Communism, nationalism is not a single, world-wide system, but is a different system in each nation. It consists essentially in collective self-glorification and in a conviction that it is right to pursue the interests of one's own nation however they may conflict with those of others. In the eighteenth century, the British proclaimed the slogan, 'Britons never shall be slaves', and proceeded to make slaves of as many non-Britons as they could. The French, shortly afterwards, proclaimed, 'Let impure blood water our furrows'—the impure blood being that of Austrians. I recently received a letter from a German explaining that 'Deutschland über alles' does not mean that Germany should rule the world, but that a German should think only of German interests. One could multiply examples indefinitely, but the phenomenon is too familiar to need further illustration.

It is rather odd that emphasis upon the merits of one's own nation should be considered a virtue. What should we think of an individual who proclaimed: 'I am morally and intellectually superior to all other individuals, and, because of this superiority, I have a right to ignore all interests except my own'? There are, no doubt, plenty of people who *feel* this way, but if they proclaim their feeling too openly, and act upon it too blatantly, they are thought ill of. When, however, a number of such individuals, constituting the population of some area, collectively make such a declaration about themselves, they are thought noble and splendid and spirited. They put up statues to each other and teach schoolchildren to admire the most blatant advocates of the national conceit.

We have become so accustomed to nationalism that it has come to seem an inherent part of human nature. History, however, does not bear out this view. In antiquity, there was hardly any nationalism except that of the Jews. In the Middle Ages, when ecclesiastics travelled freely throughout the Catholic world, their partisan feelings were centred upon their Church and not upon their nation. The nationalism of modern times has grown up, mainly, as a reaction against foreign imperialism. One may put its beginning at the time of Joan of Arc when the French were roused to collective resistance against English conquest. English nationalism began with the resistance to the Spanish Armada, and found its classic expression, a few years later, in Shakespeare. German and Russian nationalisms had their origin in resistance to Napoleon; American nationalism, in resistance to the Redcoats. Unfortunately, there is a psychologically natural dynamic which has almost invariably governed the development of nationalism. In the course of the struggle against foreign dominion, those who are fighting for freedom, not unnaturally, exaggerate their own merits and the demerits of the foreign oppressors. When they have won freedom, the beliefs formerly appropriate survive and are thought to justify foreign conquest. The appeal to group self-esteem fits in so well with people's natural propensities that it is not easily combated except where there are dissident groups having a collective self-esteem at variance with that of their nation. Nelson, before the French Revolution, instructed midshipmen that they should hate a Frenchman as they would the

Devil, and the young men to whom he commended this precept had no difficulty in accepting it and in continuing to believe it throughout twenty-two years of war.

Mankind survived the wars that have taken place hitherto, but it is doubtful whether survival will be possible in future wars. For this reason it has become imperative that sentiments promoting violent hostility between different groups must somehow be softened. I have spoken earlier of the need of tolerance as between Communist and Capitalist ideologies, and there is need of just the same kind of tolerance between nations. To bring this about will be no easy task, but it is one which will have to be undertaken before world peace can be secure and before any International Authority can win general acceptance. It is essentially an educational task. What can be done in this direction, if powerful Governments become sincerely anxious for world peace, will be our next topic of discussion.

III. EDUCATION

If the Great Powers can reach agreement that war is no longer to be an instrument of policy, one of the things that will have to be changed is education. Education in most countries is mainly in the hands of the national State and, therefore, tends to teach an outlook which is considered to be in the interests of the State concerned. It has not been thought, hitherto, that the interests of one State coincided with those of another. Nor, indeed, has this been true always, or even usually, in former times. It is the development of modern techniques, and, more especially, of nuclear weapons, that has made armed contests between States futile and has brought about an identity of interest between different countries far surpassing what was true at any earlier time. It follows that it is no longer to the interest of any country to emphasize its superiority to other countries or to cause its boys and girls to believe it invincible in war. Nor is it a good thing to present martial glory as what is, above all things, to be admired.

It is especially in the teaching of history that changes are called for. This applies not only in the lower grades, but just as much in the highest academic teaching. Hegel, who announced that he had surveyed all human history, picked out three individuals as having the most outstanding merit. They were Alexander, Caesar and Napoleon. His academic successors in his own country were more nationalistic and preferred German heroes, while French boys were being taught that heroism is French, and English boys, that it is English. This sort of thing will have to cease. I suggested long ago, though with no hope that the suggestion would be adopted, that in every country the history of that country should be taught from books written by foreigners. No doubt such books would have a bias, but it would be opposed by an opposite bias in the pupils, and the outcome might be fairly just.

But it is not only history that needs to be differently taught. Everything (except, perhaps, arithmetic) should be taught as part of the progress of Man, and as a series of steps in the conquest of obstacles with which he has been faced and is still faced. There is a danger that, in ceasing to emphasize wars, teaching will cease to be exciting, but this danger can be entirely avoided by emphasizing exciting contests with difficulties and dangers other than those of war.

There are, one may say, three great spheres of contest involved in the gradual approach of man towards wisdom.[1] There are the contests with nature, the contests between men, and the contests within a man's own self. Each of these has its own history and its own importance.

The contests with nature, which begin with the problem of securing food, lead on, step by step, to the scientific understanding of natural processes and the technical power of utilizing sources of energy. It is in this sphere that man's greatest triumphs have hitherto been won, and it is likely that many even greater triumphs will be achieved in the not very distant future. The story of man's increasing mastery over nature is inherently exciting, and is felt to be so by the young, except when it is taught in schools. It could be just as exciting in schools if teachers were adequate and the methods prescribed were appropriate. Love of adventure, which hitherto has been too often an incentive to war, can find abundant openings in the sphere of natural knowledge. Explorations in America, Africa, the Poles and the Himalayas could all be made vivid by being shown in moving pictures on the screen. The future possibilities of space-travel, which are now left mainly to unfounded fantasy, could be more soberly treated without ceasing to be interesting and could show to even the most adventurous of the young that a world without war need not be a world without adventurous and hazardous glory. To this kind of contest there is no limit. Each victory is only a prelude to another, and no boundaries can be set to rational hope.

[1] See my *New Hopes for a Changing World.*

The second kind of conflict, namely, that of men with other men, when it consists of armed combat between groups, is the one with which we have been especially concerned in this book. It is one which, on any rational survey, must be ended if human progress is to continue. I am not contending, as a full-fledged pacifist might, that contests between different groups of men have never in the past served a useful purpose. I do not think that this would be true. It has happened over and over again that barbarians have descended from the mountains upon fruitful plains and civilized cities and have done vast damage before civilized forces could curb their destructive vigour. But the increased area occupied by civilized men and the increased power which modern weapons have conferred upon them, has reduced to very small proportions the danger of such cataclysms as the destruction of the Roman Empire by the barbarians. It is not now barbarians who constitute the danger. On the contrary, it is those who are in the forefront of civilization. It should be one of the tasks of education to make vivid in the minds of the young both the merits of a civilized way of life and the needless dangers to which it is exposed by the survival of competitive ideals which have become archaic.

In the great majority of human beings, there is, in addition to outer conflicts, an inner conflict between different impulses and desires which are not mutually compatible. Systems of morality are intended to deal with such conflicts and, to a certain degree, they are often successful. But I think that the changing conditions of human life make changes of moral outlook necessary from time to time. One such change, which is especially necessary at the present time, is that each individual

83

should learn to view groups of human beings other than his own as possible co-operators, rather than as probable competitors. But this whole subject is a very large one, and to pursue it would take us too far from our central theme.

What the world most needs, in education as in other departments of human life, is the substitution of hope for fear, and the realization of the splendid thing that life may be if the human family co-operatively will permit itself to realize its best potentialities.

Unilateral Disarmament

Some of my critics have laid stress upon the fact that in certain hypothetical circumstances I should think either the East or the West well advised if it disarmed unilaterally. My critics have omitted my provisos and have spoken as if I had advocated a disarmament policy for the West alone, and not equally for the East, in the circumstances supposed. My critics are not wholly to blame for this. I have been led into a purely academic issue as if it were one of practical politics. Everybody knows that neither the United States nor the USSR will disarm unilaterally. The question whether either would be wise to do so is therefore no more than an exercise in theoretical ethics. Speaking practically, and not theoretically, what I advocate is that methods should be sought of, first, lessening the East-West tension and then negotiating agreements on vexed questions on the basis of giving no net advantage to either side. Such negotiations, if they are to be satisfactory, must include the mutual renunciation of nuclear weapons with an adequate system of inspection.

It is true that I advocate practically, and not only theoretically, the abandonment of the H-bomb by Britain and the prevention of the spread of H-bombs to Powers other than the United States and the USSR. I do not consider that unilateral renunciation of British H-bombs would have any measurable effect upon the balance of power, and I do consider that the acquisition of H-bombs by many Powers will greatly increase the danger of a nuclear war. This makes the question of British renunciation of H-bombs quite distinct from that of general unilateral disarmament by one of the two camps.

The question at issue between my critics and myself arises only if all attempts at negotiation fail. My critics speak as though I wished the Government of the United States to announce that it is prepared to give way at all points, and suggest that I have no such wish as regards the Soviet Government. I think this question is quite unreal since, whatever might be the part of ideal wisdom, it is certain that neither side will surrender completely to the other. However, since the question is considered important, I will do my best to re-state my opinion more unmistakably.

To eliminate emotional factors, I shall speak of two Power Blocs, A and B, leaving it completely undetermined which of them is Communist and which anti-Communist. The argument proceeds on the hypothesis that, if there is a war between the two blocs, the human race will be exterminated. It further supposes a situation in which one of the two blocs is so fanatical that it prefers the ending of mankind to a rational compromise. In such a situation, I think that the less fanatical bloc, if it had the welfare of mankind in view, would prefer concession to warfare. I should say this equally to both sides.

There are those in both camps who think that the extermination of the human race would be a smaller evil than the victory of the 'enemy'. I regard this view, whether held by A or by B, as insane. My Western critics and some of Mr Krushchev's supporters agree when it is held by one side, but not when it is held by the other. The opinion which I have expressed, that it would be better to yield than to indulge in a nuclear war, is addressed to both parties equally, and I do not think it likely to have any more influence on the one side than on the other.

The argument that you cannot negotiate successfully if you announce in advance that, if pressed, you will yield, is entirely valid. If I were the Government of either A or B, I should make no such an announcement. But this has no bearing on the purely academic question of what it would be wise to do if the completely desperate situation arose. I must, however, once more insist that the view in favour of avoiding nuclear warfare even at great cost is one which applies to both sides equally and which, as far as I can judge, is no more unlikely to be adopted by one side than by the other. It is entirely unjust to regard the opinions that I have expressed as more useful to the one side than to the other. In fact, I have proclaimed my views to both sides equally, and my advocacy of them has been published as widely in Communist countries as in the United States.

I should like to correct a misunderstanding promoted, I think, by a report of an interview in which only a small part of my thought was expressed. I think that, with wise statesmanship on the part of the West and of the East, it will not be at all difficult to avoid both nuclear war and surrender. What I advocate in practice, and not as the outcome of an artificial logical dilemma, is a conclusion of agreements between East and West admitting the inevitability of co-existence and the disastrous futility of war. I wish both sides to realize that war cannot achieve anything that either side desires, and that, in consequence, points in dispute can only be settled by negotiation.

Many of my critics, though they are in the habit of proclaiming that they value freedom, on this point deceive themselves. They do not think that those who prefer life rather than death, even under Communism or under Capitalism, as the case may be, should be free to choose the alternative that they prefer. Not only the inhabitants of Communist nations—or of Capitalist nations—but the inhabitants of all the uncommitted nations are denied by them the most elementary freedom, which is freedom to choose survival. The view that No World is better than a Communist world, or that No World is better than a Capitalist World, is one that is difficult to refute by abstract arguments, but I think that those who hold it should question their right to impose their opinion upon those who do not hold it by the infliction of the death penalty upon all of them. This is an extreme form of religious persecution, going far beyond anything that has been advocated in previous human history.

Inconsistency?

Opponents of my recent activities in the campaign against H-bomb warfare have brought up what they consider to be an inconsistency on my part and have used statements that I made ten years ago to impair the force of the statements that I have made more recently. I should like to clear up this matter once for all.

At a time when America alone possessed the atom bomb and when the American Government was advocating what was known as the Baruch Proposal, the aim of which was to internationalize all the uses of atomic energy, I thought the American proposal both wise and generous. It seemed to me that the Baruch scheme, if adopted, would prevent an atomic arms race, the appalling dangers of which were evident to all informed opinion in the Western World. For a time it seemed possible that the USSR would agree to this scheme, since Russia had everything to gain by agreeing and nothing to lose. Unfortunately, Stalin's suspicious nature made him think that there was some trap, and Russia decided to produce her own atomic weapons. I thought, at that time, that it would be worth while to bring pressure to bear upon Russia and even, if necessary, to go so far as to threaten war on the sole issue of the internationalizing of atomic weapons. My aim, then as now, was to prevent a war in which both sides possessed the power of producing world-wide disaster. Western statesmen, however, confident of the supposed technical superiority of the West, believed that there was no danger of Russia achieving equality with the non-Communist world in the field of nuclear warfare. Their confidence in this respect has turned out to have been mistaken. It follows that, if nuclear war is now to be prevented, it must be by new methods and not by those which could have been employed ten years ago.

My critics seem to think that, if you have once advocated a certain policy, you should continue to advocate it after all the circumstances have changed. This is quite absurd. If a man gets into a train with a view to reaching a certain destination and on the way the train breaks down, you will not consider the man guilty of an inconsistency if he gets out of the train and employs other means of reaching his destination. In like manner, a person who advocates a certain policy in certain circumstances will advocate a quite different policy in different circumstances.

I have never been a complete pacifist and have at no time maintained that all who wage war are to be condemned. I have held the view, which I should have thought was that of common sense, that some wars have been justified and others not. What makes the peculiarity of the present situation is that, if a great war should break out, the belligerents on either side and the neutrals would be all, equally, defeated. This is a new situation and means that war cannot still be used as an instrument of policy. It is true that the threat of war can still be used, but only by a lunatic. Unfortunately, some people *are* lunatics, and, not long ago, there were such lunatics in command of a powerful State. We cannot be sure this will not happen again and, if it does, it will produce a disaster compared with which the horrors achieved by Hitler were a flea-bite. The world at present is balanced in unstable equilibrium upon a sharp edge. To achieve stability, new methods are required, and it is these new methods that those who think as I do are attempting to urge upon the East and upon the West.

I do not deny that the policy that I have advocated has changed from time to time. It has changed as circumstances have changed. To achieve a single purpose, sane men adapt their policies to the circumstances. Those who do not are insane.

Though I do not admit inconsistency, I should not be wholly sincere if I did not admit that my mood and feelings have undergone a change somewhat deeper than that resulting from strategic considerations alone. The awful prospect of the extermination of the human race, if not in the next war, then in the next but one or the next but two, is so sobering to any imagination which has seriously contemplated it as to demand very fundamental fresh thought on the whole subject not only of international relations but of human life and its capabilities. If you were quarrelling with a man about some issue that both you and he had thought important just at the moment when a sudden hurricane threatened to destroy you both and the whole neighbourhood, you would probably forget the quarrel. I think what is important at present is to make mankind aware of the hurricane and forgetful of the issue which had been producing strife.

Common Sense and Nuclear Warfare

I know it is difficult after spending many years and much eloquence on the evils of Communism or Capitalism, as the case may be, to see this issue as one of relative unimportance. But, although this is difficult, it is what both the Communist Rulers and the men who shape the policy of the West will have to achieve if mankind is to survive. To make such a realization possible is the purpose of the policy which I now advocate.

About the Author

BERTRAND ARTHUR WILLIAM RUSSELL *received the Nobel Prize for Literature in 1950. He is the grandson of Lord John Russell, who was thrice Prime Minister and British Foreign Secretary under Queen Victoria. During more than half a century many books have flowed from his pen—books that have shown him to be the most brilliant of philosophers, the most profound of mathematicians, and the most lucid of popularizers. His most recent major works are* A History of Western Philosophy, *published in 1945;* Human Knowledge: Its Scope and Limits *(1948);* Authority and the Individual *(1949);* Unpopular Essays *(1951),* that grossly mistitled book; *New Hopes for a Changing World *(1952);* The Impact of Science on Society *(1953);* Human Society in Ethics and Politics *(1955);* Portraits from Memory *(1956); and* Why I Am Not a Christian *(1957).*

SIMON AND SCHUSTER PAPERBACKS

For people who want to know more about science,
philosophy, the arts and history in the making

THE ART OF DRAMATIC WRITING by Lajos Egri	$1.45
ATOMIC POWER by the Editors of *Scientific American*	1.45
AUTOMATIC CONTROL by the Editors of *Scientific American*	1.45
THE CAUSES OF WORLD WAR THREE by C. Wright Mills	1.50
COMMON SENSE AND NUCLEAR WARFARE by Bertrand Russell	1.00
DESIGNING FOR PEOPLE by Henry Dreyfuss	1.95
ENJOYMENT OF LAUGHTER by Max Eastman	1.50
THE GREEK PASSION by Nikos Kazantzakis	1.95
HISTORY OF WESTERN PHILOSOPHY by Bertrand Russell	2.25
HOW NOT TO WRITE A PLAY by Walter Kerr	1.45
HOW TO READ A BOOK by Mortimer J. Adler	1.75
IS ANYBODY LISTENING? by William H. Whyte, Jr.	1.25
A LAYMAN'S GUIDE TO PSYCHIATRY AND PSYCHOANALYSIS by Eric Berne, M.D.	1.50
LIVES IN SCIENCE by the Editors of *Scientific American*	1.45
LOVEJOY'S COLLEGE GUIDE (5th Ed.) by Clarence E. Lovejoy	2.50
MEN OF MUSIC by Wallace Brockway and Herbert Weinstock	1.95
THE NEW ASTRONOMY by the Editors of *Scientific American*	1.45
NEW CHEMISTRY by the Editors of *Scientific American*	1.45
THE OPEN MIND by J. Robert Oppenheimer	1.00
PEACE WITH RUSSIA? by Averell Harriman	1.00
THE PHYSICS AND CHEMISTRY OF LIFE by the Editors of *Scientific American*	1.45
THE PLANET EARTH by the Editors of *Scientific American*	1.45
PLANT LIFE by the Editors of *Scientific American*	1.45
THE PLEASURES OF PHILOSOPHY by Will Durant	1.75
THE PUBLIC ARTS by Gilbert Seldes	1.50
READING I'VE LIKED by Clifton Fadiman	2.25
THE RELIGIONS OF AMERICA edited by Leo Rosten	1.50
THE SCIENTIFIC AMERICAN READER by the Editors of *Scientific American*	2.25
TELEVISION PLAYS by Paddy Chayefsky	1.75
THURBER COUNTRY by James Thurber	1.45
TWENTIETH-CENTURY BESTIARY by the Editors of *Scientific American*	1.45
THE UNIVERSE by the Editors of *Scientific American*	1.45
UNPOPULAR ESSAYS by Bertrand Russell	1.00
VASARI'S LIVES OF THE ARTISTS edited by Betty Burroughs	1.95
THE WORLDLY PHILOSOPHERS by Robert L. Heilbroner	1.50
WHAT IS SCIENCE? edited by James R. Newman	1.95
WITH MALICE TOWARD SOME by Margaret Halsey	1.45
ZORBA THE GREEK by Nikos Kazantzakis	1.75